Julia Seal

REAL SUPERHEROES

For
Andrew
Hannah
Ruth
Tennelle
Jean
Ed & Ari
Brendan
Wendy
Elmie
Beth
Pippa
and
essential
workers
everywhere

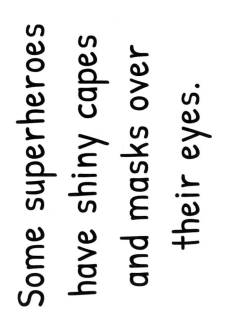

Some superheroes have shiny capes and masks over their eyes.

They fly around, awaiting the sound of
"HELP ME! HELP ME! HELP ME!" cries.

They have super-strength...

and laser eyes...

a trusty sidekick, too.

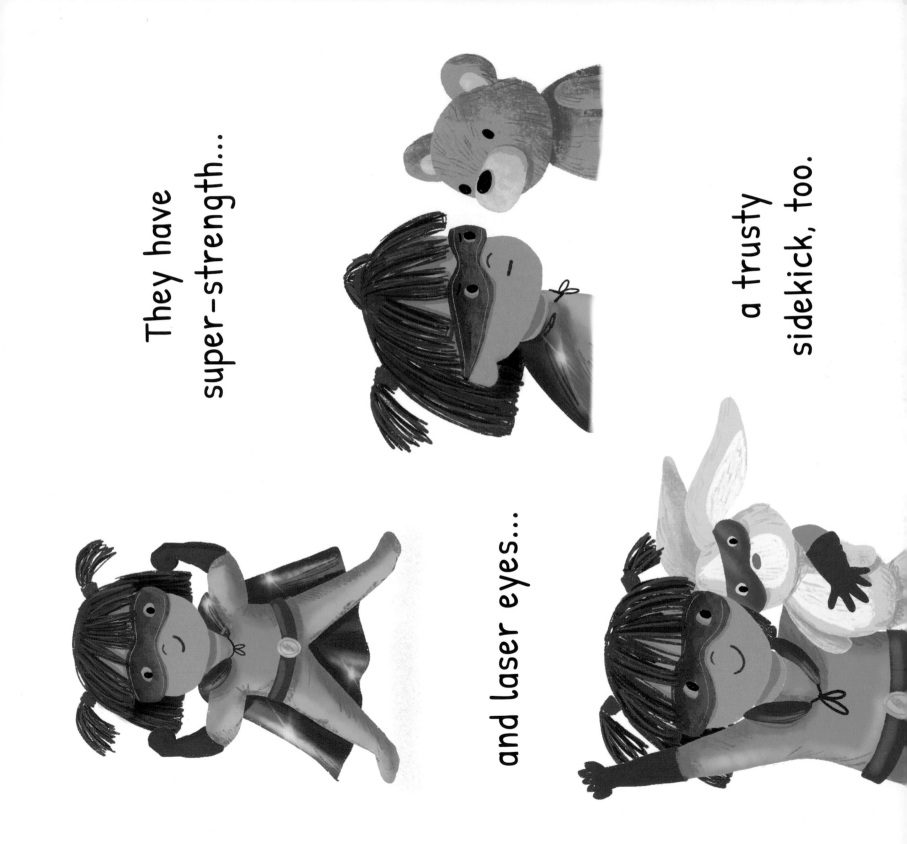

But how many of these superheroes
have ever rescued you?

No, I want to be a real superhero,
the kind that does exist.

The sort that comes and helps you when you fall and break your wrist.

The type that will
come running
when you're lost
and all alone.

They answer people's cries for help when you call them on the phone.

Not all heroes have fancy cars.
Some drive in flashy trucks.
They fight fire to keep us safe.
We wish them lots of luck.

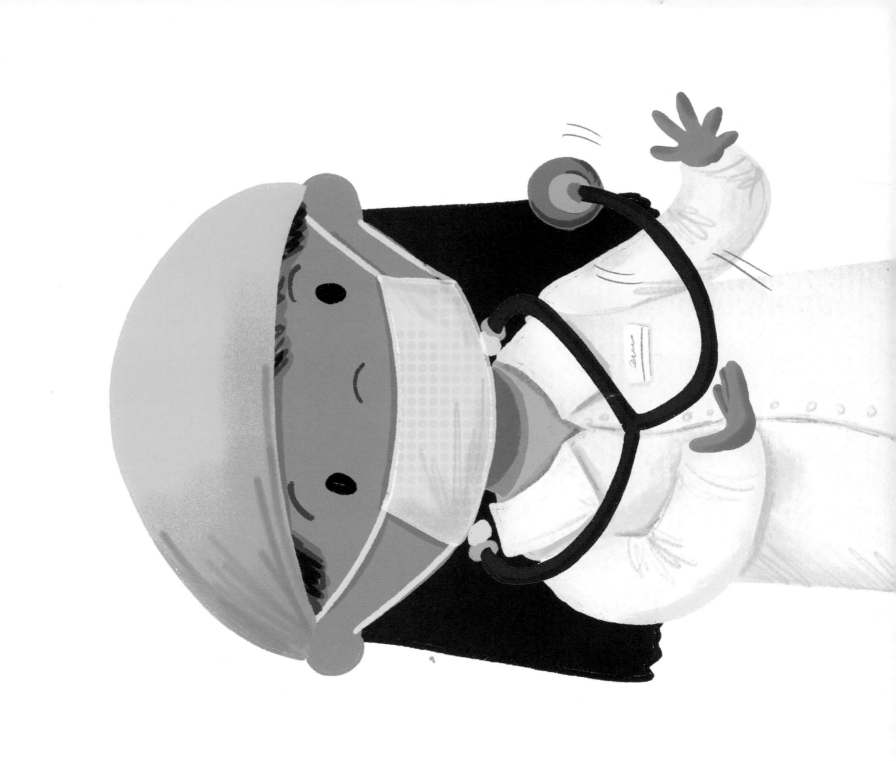

Some superheroes have stethoscopes
as well as colored masks.

These tools are not as swishy as a cape,
but they help with tricky tasks.

Some rid the world of waste
by emptying all the bins.

They really do save the planet
by recycling glass and cans.

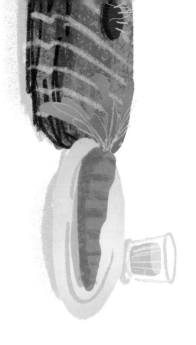

And don't forget those heroes
with the superpower to care.

They often go unnoticed,
but I sure am glad they're there.

Through storms and sickness,
when hope seems gone...

Real superheroes must carry on.

So when I grow up I don't want a cape,
it'd just get in the way.
But I still want to save people
and help them every day.

I'll teach the
world what's
right or wrong.

I'll be brave... I'll be strong.

while out on patrol I'll keep people safer.

I'll keep the shelves stocked with toilet paper.

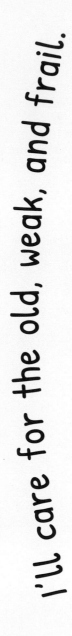

I'll care for the old, weak, and frail.

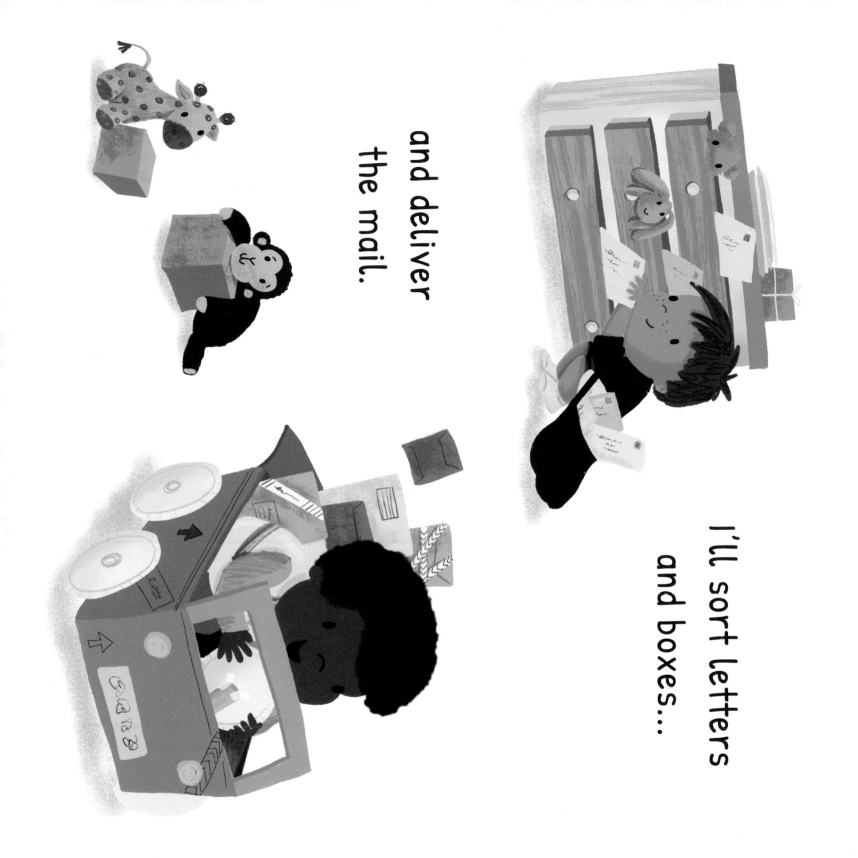

and deliver
the mail.

I'll sort letters
and boxes...

I'll make sure people are well fed.

I'll be there at their hospital bed.

I'm thankful for these superheroes,
working day and night.

As long as there are real superheroes,
I know we'll be alright.

Julia Seal

Julia is an author-illustrator from a small village in England. She knew from the age of five what she wanted to do for a living—draw pictures!

After studying Graphic Design and Illustration, Julia got a job making greeting cards, where she came home each day covered in glitter. After this, she managed to land her dream job of creating children's books, and hasn't looked back since. She's illustrated more than 70 books over the past 9 years!

Julia has recently started writing books and gets her inspiration from things going on around her. She keeps a little book of funny quotes and overheard snippets of conversations that often turn into stories. Her two children also provide endless inspiration.

Julia would like to say a special thank you to the Teachers of Box C of E Primary School.

Penguin Random House

Produced for DK by Collaborate Agency

Editor Sally Beets
US Editor Lori Hand
Designer Brandie Tully-Scott

Jacket Coordinator Issy Walsh
Publishing Manager Francesca Young
Publishing Director Sarah Larter
Production Editor Nikoleta Parasaki
Production Controller Ena Matagic

First American Edition, 2020
Published in the United States by DK Publishing
1450 Broadway, Suite 801, New York, NY 10018

Copyright © 2020 Dorling Kindersley Limited
DK, a Division of Penguin Random House LLC
21 22 23 24 25 10 9 8 7 6 5 4 3 2 1
002-323470-Apr/2021

A catalog record for this book
is available from the Library of Congress.
ISBN 978-0-7440-3701-2

DK books are available at special discounts when purchased in bulk for sales promotions, premiums, fund-raising, or educational use. For details, contact: DK Publishing Special Markets, 1450 Broadway, Suite 801, New York, NY 10018
SpecialSales@dk.com

Printed and bound in China

MIX
Paper from
responsible sources
FSC™ C018179

For the curious
www.dk.com